About this book

Many children have difficulty puzzling out letters because they are abstract symbols. Letterland's worldwide success is all about its enduring characters who give these symbols life and stop them from being abstract. In this book we meet Munching Mike. His story is carefully designed to emphasise the sounds that the letter 'M' makes in words. This definitive, original story book is an instant collector's classic, making learning fun for a new generation of readers.

A TEMPLAR BOOK

This edition published in the UK in 2008 by Templar Publishing
an imprint of The Templar Company plc,
The Granary, North Street, Dorking, Surrey, RH4 1DN, UK
www.templarco.co.uk

First published by Hamlyn Publishing, 1985
Devised and produced by The Templar Company plc

ISBN 978-1-84011-761-5

Printed in China

Munching Mike's Mistake

Written by
Keith Nicholson & Lyn Wendon

Illustrated by
Jane Launchbury

templar publishing

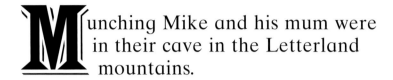

Munching Mike and his mum were in their cave in the Letterland mountains.

Munching Mike's Mum was cross.
She had just tripped over Mike's coloured marbles... for the third time that day.

"I've told you a million time not to leave your marbles lying about!" she cried.

"Oh, but I didn't mean to," said Mike.
"It was a mistake."

His mum sighed. "This cave is too small," she said. "It's time we moved somewhere bigger."

"Move?!!" said the metal monster in amazement, "but where to?"

"I know just the place," said his mum. "It's a big old mine shaft somewhere on Misty Mountain. The Mountain Moose told me all about it. You go on and find it, and I'll meet you there."

Munching Mike liked the idea of moving to a new home.

"But wait!" he said suddenly. "I haven't had my mid-morning snack yet. I can't go until I've eaten!"

"Oh yes you can," said his mum, and the look on her face made Mike decide to set off at once.

The first place Munching Mike came to was a meadow full of mushrooms. It led towards the Misty Mountain, and it looked delicious. So he munched his way right across it. When he reached the other side he felt a little bit better.

"I wonder what I can eat next?" he thought to himself.

Then he saw a sign. He sniffed it. Yes, it was made of metal. So he ate it in one mouthful.

"Much better!" he muttered. Crunchy metal was his favourite food.

Next, Munching Mike came to a long road. It was the Mountain Motorway. Now he could move much faster.

Soon he was rolling along so fast that he almost missed his next meal!
It was another tasty sign.

He swerved and snatched a mouthful.
"Even munchier!" he said to himself.

Then he raced on along the motorway.

At the end of the motorway
Munching Mike found a track.
It led higher up the mountain.
Beside the track were some bits of an
old machine.

Munching Mike's mouth watered.

"Mmmmm!" he said out loud, and
munched his way through the whole lot!

"Almost as good as a main meal!"
he said when he had finished.

Soon Munching Mike came to another sign. It was a map of the Misty Mountains.

He sniffed the sign.
"Mmmmm, this smells very tasty," he said.

Before he could stop himself, Munching Mike had taken an enormous mouthful out of it.

"Oh help!" he said. "That was a mistake. I've just munched up the map.
Now I don't know where the mine is!"

Just to make things worse, Munching Mike was STILL hungry.

Map of the
Misty
Mountains

YOU ARE
HERE

N

Mike slowly rolled on up the track. A mist was settling on the mountain. Munching Mike could hardly see anything in front of him.

He began to wonder if he would ever find the old mine, or anything else to eat!

Munching Mike didn't mean to think about food, but he couldn't help it. He thought of the crunchy meals his mum always made for him.

Munching Mike began to feel miserable.

"I think I've made a mess of things," he mumbled. "What do I do now?" Then he remembered his mum saying, "If you ever get scared, take a deep breath,"

So he did, and he felt a lot better.

A moment later he let out his breath with a whoosh. To his great surprise his hot breath blew a hole in the mist.

And what did he see???

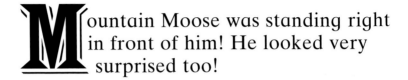

Mountain Moose was standing right in front of him! He looked very surprised too!

"What, may I ask, do you think you are doing, blowing hot air at me like that?" asked the Moose.

"I didn't mean to," said Mike, and quickly added for the third time that day, "it was a mistake…"

Mountain Moose nodded wisely. "I supposed you were looking for the old mine."

"Yes," said Mike. "I have to meet my mum at the mine."

"Never mind," said Mountain Moose calmly. "Just try blowing again." Then Mike saw where he was.

He was standing right outside the entrance to the old mine. There was even a sign that said 'Mountain Mine Entrance'.

There was another sign too.
"I knew your mum wanted to move in," said the Moose, "so I put up a sign specially for you."

"Marvellous!" cried Mike.
"My mum will be so pleased!"

Sure enough, at that very moment his mum arrived. The two metal monsters looked happily at the sign outside their new home.

It said 'Monster Mansion'.
Munching Mike sniffed it closely.
"Mmmmm, another metal sign,"
he murmured. But he stopped himself from taking a mouthful. "I don't think I'll make that mistake again," he said.

Then he added proudly, "This mine is mine!"

"You mean ours!" said his mum.
"Oh yes," said Mike with a grin.
"My mistake!"

Monster
Mansion

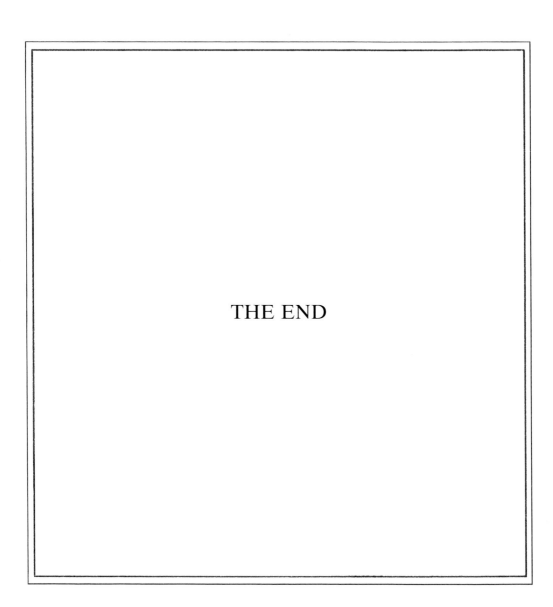

THE END